ANYONE CAN WIN SWEEPSTAKES

BY R. L. PELSON

1980 Edition
Ninth Printing

R & D SERVICES
P. O. BOX 644,
DES MOINES, IOWA 50303

FOREWORD

It is possible for anyone to win sweepstakes and win consistently! All it takes is an organized, systematic approach, a planned method of entering, and a little luck!

Most people half-heartedly submit a few entries in one or two sweepstakes and, not overwhelmed with instant success, soon give up. My method of winning--and it can be yours too--is described in detail in the following pages. All you need to do is devote a little time, acquire the know-how, and invest in postage. By following the methods in this book, I won 42 prizes in a period of 18 months. All of them were not big prizes, but it's fun winning the smaller prizes knowing that you're in there with a chance to win the big one. My prizes included three television sets (one of them in color), kitchen appliances, cameras, a bicycle and other such items.

Don't confuse current sweepstakes with "contests." In contests, you must do something skillful such as completing a statement in 25 words or less, or making up the last line of a jingle. Sweepstakes take no such skill. They are simply a drawing to determine the winners. In most sweepstakes, the entries are put in a large barrel from which the winners are drawn by someone who is blindfolded. This is called a "blindfold drawing."

In the past five years or so, there has been an abundance of sweepstakes. Usually, you can find 15 or more going on at any one time. Look in almost any magazine and you will find one or two sweepstakes with fabulous prizes being advertised. Cash, cars, television sets, world trips--you name it! There is no trick. The prizes are given away to SOMEONE, and, as the old saying goes, it might as well be you! Sweepstakes have received an added boost to their already plentiful supply. Since cigarettes cannot be advertised on TV any more, many tobacco companies are turning to sweepstakes as a means of promotion, and they are giving away fabulous, BIG prizes by the hundreds.

You do not have to sit back and watch someone else win these big prizes because you do not know how to go about entering or because you figure you don't have a chance, or because you've never won anything in your life!

This book will take you step-by-step through the complete sweepstakes process. In simple, easy-to-understand instructions, it will tell you secrets and methods that others have used to win, and to win consistently! You will find tips, shortcuts, methods of obtaining cheaper supplies, how to make block letters, questions and answers, plus much more.

So get busy, read this book and start your sweepstakes entries rolling in. Get some supplies--envelopes, 3" x 5" pads of paper, postage, pens, and you're ready to go. The more entries that the sweepstakes receive, the more convincing it will be to them that sweepstakes are a successful means of promotion. And the more sweepstakes, the better chance to win.

FOLLOWING OFFICIAL RULES

It cannot be stressed too much that it is important to follow exactly the official rules for the sweepstakes you are entering. Each sweepstakes has its own set of rules to be followed exactly or you will be disqualified. The best way to tell you how to do this is to list the actual rules of a recent sweepstakes, then to take you step-by-step through them.

RULE NO. 1 On an official entry blank or on a 3" x 5" piece of paper, print your name, address and zip code and the name and address of your dealer (if any).

If you have the official entry blank, fine--use it. If you don't, a 3" x 5" piece of paper is perfectly acceptable. It should be plain paper, not ruled. You can buy 3" x 5" pads of paper in your discount or stationery store. You can use this same size in most sweepstakes for your block letters, too. The rules state PRINT your name, and it means just that. Do not use script. Make sure that you include your zip code, and the name and address of your dealer. In most cases, your dealer will probably be the local store that carries the product. Write the store's name, not the man's name.

RULE NO. 2 With each entry, send 2 empty (brand name) packages or the "(brand name of product)" printed in block letters on a 3" x 5" piece of paper. Enter as often as you wish, but each entry must be mailed in a separate envelope. Entries must be postmarked by (date) and received by (date).

This rule is about the "qualifier" that you have to enclose with your entries. As it states, you can send in EITHER the box tops or labels themselves or the product name printed by you in block letters on a separate 3" x 5" piece of paper. As I will state many times, block letter qualifiers are perfectly acceptable to use. You DO NOT need to purchase the product in order to win. See the section on block letters for a description on how they are made. If the rules state to print them on a SEPARATE piece of paper, do so, do not put them on the same 3" x 5" piece of paper that you used for your name and address. The "Enter as often as you wish" statement is the one we like to see. With that rule, we can submit as many entries as desired. Just make sure that each entry is mailed in a separate envelope. About the closing date for the sweepstakes: most will give two dates, one for the postmark deadline, and one for the received deadline. However, some sweepstakes give just one closing date, so determine whether it's to be a postmark deadline or a received-by deadline. Save a few of your entries for the very last day.

If you live in a large city and deposit your entries at a post office where it is picked up hourly, 24 hours a day, don't wait until midnight to deposit them and expect them to be postmarked with that day's date. While cancelling machines change their dates at midnight, you must deposit your entries a few hours earlier as it may take that long to process and cancel them after they are picked up from the collection box.

RULE NO. 3 Winners will be determined by a random drawing, conducted by an independent judging organization whose decisions are final.

Most sponsors leave the conduct of sweepstakes--the drawing of the winners--to independent companies who specialize in this. Two such are the D. L. Blair Co. of Blair, Nebraska and Robert Scott Associates of New York City. These companies are specialists in this field, more experienced and equipped to handle large volumes of mail. More about how winners are chosen later.

RULE NO. 4 Prizes are non-transferable. No substitutes for prizes offered. Only one prize to a family. The odds of winning will be determined by the number of entries received. ALL prizes are to be awarded.

This rule is pretty much self-explanatory. On the "only one prize to a family" rule, some sweepstakes say this and some don't. If it isn't stated, it may be entirely possible for more than one member of the family to win a prize in the same sweepstakes. It has happened in my family, but in most cases, it is usually the smaller prizes which are so won.

RULE NO. 5 Local, state and federal taxes, if any, are the responsibility of the winner.

Again, this rule is self-explanatory. For it simply means that you, and not the sponsors, must pay the taxes, if any. See my section on taxes for more on this subject.

RULE NO. 6 Sweepstakes open to residents of the continental United States and Hawaii only. Entrants must be 21 years of age or older. Employees and their families of the sponsor company, its advertising agency, and judging organization are not eligible. Void wherever prohibited or restricted by law. All federal, state, and local laws and regulations apply. NO PURCHASE REQUIRED.

This rule is pretty well standard in all the sweepstakes, except for the age restriction of 21 years. This particular sweepstakes was sponsored by a cigarette company. These rules closed with the stipulation NO PURCHASE REQUIRED. This is the regulation. If you had to purchase their product, it would be more of a lottery than a sweepstakes and would be illegal. In a contest, as opposed to sweepstakes, you may be required to purchase the product. A contest involves skill such as completing a statement in 25 words or less or completing the last line of a jingle. In the 1950's, contests were big, but in recent years, they have largely given way to random-drawn sweepstakes where no such skill is required.

When you receive the official rules, immediately take a red pencil and underline the important facts, such as plain paper size, block letters permissible and the closing date. After you have completed your entries but prior to stuffing and sealing, DOUBLE CHECK each and every item on the rules, making sure you have followed them exactly. There will always be a certain percentage of entries received that will be disqualified because of the violation of one or more rules. Don't let this happen to your entries.

QUALIFIERS

A qualifier, in sweepstakes terminology, is the box top, label or other proof of purchase that you usually have to enclose with your entries to "qualify" for winning. It can also be a plain piece of paper, usually 3" x 5", on which you have printed the product name in block letters. Many people think they must enclose the actual label or purchase the sponsor's product in order to have a better chance of winning. One of the most frequently asked questions is, "Can you really win by writing the sponsor's name in block letters on a 3" x 5" piece of plain paper?" Let me say right now in the most certain of terms! Yes, you can win with plain paper!! You do not need to purchase the sponsor's product in order to win!!! In fact, Federal and U. S. Postal Service laws prohibit sweepstakes from requiring that you purchase the product. This would be a lottery and against regulation. I can verify this myself as I have won many prizes with plain paper qualifiers. In fact, I almost exclusively use plain paper qualifiers, rarely using the actual proof of purchase. Other people have reported in various sweepstakes magazines that they have won prizes, at ALL LEVELS, with plain paper qualifiers.

This doesn't necessarily mean that I never purchase the sponsor's product. If I have need of the commodity, I may buy it, unless it's something like an automobile! After all, the sponsors are giving away prizes to sell more of their products, and I feel that usually it won't hurt anyone to buy one can of a certain brand of beans, one box of soap, a carton of the sponsor's cigarettes if he smokes, or whatever. However, even when I do this, I rarely bother to include the proof of purchase with my entries. I still use plain paper qualifiers because it's easier and less bulky for mailing.

You may wonder if you would increase your chances by using real qualifiers although you know it is possible to use plain qualifiers. Stop wondering! The answer is no. Thousands and thousands of entries are received in these big sweepstakes. The judging organizations do not open the entries until after they have been drawn. Hence, it is impossible to increase your chances by enclosing the actual qualifier.

HOW TO MAKE BLOCK LETTERS

In the majority of sweepstakes, as a substitute for enclosing the actual product label or box top, the rules will state that you can print the product name in block letters on a 3" x 5" piece of plain paper. There has been much confusion regarding the nature of block letters. Here are actual examples.

BLOCK BLOCK

Both of these are block letters, both of them are acceptable and both of them have won prizes. However, the first example is the easiest to make as you don't have to worry with double lines. This is the kind I use. I make my block letters with a felt tip marker pen. These pens make attractive block letters and work fast. I use the thin felt tip markers. They make a thicker line than a ball point but still thin enough for ease of printing. However, even the thinnest of ball point pens would be perfectly all right to use.

Don't get the idea that your block letters have to be as neat as the following examples. They don't. Do make them as legible as possible and make sure that you are spelling the product name correctly!

A B C D E F G H I J

K L M N O P Q R

S T U V W X Y Z

ALL ABOUT ENVELOPES

While prizes at all levels have been given to entries sent in small as well as large envelopes, I prefer using the large #10 business size, 4¼" x 9½". The idea is that with the larger envelope size, the more envelope there is to "draw to." The #10 size has more volume than the regular 6 3/4" size. So, you might say that you have a better chance of having a winning envelope drawn if it is larger rather than smaller.

The best way to buy envelopes is in large quantities in order to take advantage of discount prices. Wait until you see them on sale at discount stores, then buy in quantity. You can obtain them this way for about $5.00 per thousand, instead of the regular price of about $10.00 per 1,000. An even cheaper way is to call around to various printing shops and wholesale envelope houses. Often, they will have misprints and seconds available at a fraction of the regular price. Sometimes, they are even free! They may have a return address on them but that does no harm if you put your own address label over it. Another way to get them for practically nothing is to obtain them from companies going out of business. I recently bought 10,000 at $1.00 per thousand. Make sure you store your envelopes in a cool, dry place or you may end up with all the flaps stuck shut.

There is one group of sweepstakes enthusiasts which uses a method of entering sweepstakes which I call the "colorful" method. They submit colorful entries, using large, weirdly-colored and odd-sized envelopes, decorate their entries, etc. The leader in this type of method is Bill Danch, a writer, who lives in Southern California. He is sometimes called the "Contest King." Over the last several years, he says that he has won some 2,000 sweepstakes and contest prizes, and I have no doubt that it is true. In fact, he has appeared in several TV shows because of his prize-winning abilities. He was on "I've Got a Secret" and the "ABC News." I watched him myself one day on a segment of "60 Minutes" on CBS. It was a very interesting, informative show. He also had a feature-length story written about him in the Los Angeles Times, and a wire service picked up his story and circulated it nation-wide.

However, Danch has stirred up something of a controversy in contesting circles. After seeing him on TV and reading about him in their newspapers, some people have said they don't see how his methods work. They flatly refuse to believe that they do work. They say that he would have won all those prizes whether he used his "methods" or not. Further, even if they do work, they say, once all the publicity got around, everybody would copy his method and the method would stop working.

To probe these allegations, I wrote to Bill Danch about one year AFTER all the publicity about his methods. I asked him if he was still using the methods and if he was still winning. I wrote:

> "Does your use of color and fancy envelopes really work? There is a lot of controversy among sweepstakes enthusiasts regarding this. Some say it definitely works; others say that it is "hogwash."

To which Mr. Danch promptly replied:

> "Odd about color and decorating envelopes. I win all the time with this method, yet I keep hearing how it won't work. This month alone, I won six prizes ranging from a colored television set and electric dishwasher to hockey sets. I win more often, however, using names of relatives than by using my own name because I think the judges know too much about me and my wins. The last sizeable contest I won--with colored envelopes, yet!!--was a trip which came to nearly $3,000 in total value including $500 for spending money. This was only six months ago, mind you!"

Mr. Danch has written a book about his prizewinning methods and on winning sweepstakes and contests in general. It is called "HOW I WON 2,000 SWEEPSTAKES PRIZE CONTESTS." If you would be interested in reading it and trying for yourself some of these "colorful" methods, you may be able to buy it from the dealer you purchased this booklet from. If not, contact the publisher, R & D Services, PO Box 644, Des Moines, Iowa 50303.

HOW MANY ENTRIES TO SUBMIT?

It is known that top prizes have been won with just a single entry. However, the beauty of most of today's sweepstakes is that you can enter as many times as you wish. That is the way in which you increase your odds. Most sweepstakes worth entering should have between 25 and 200 entries. This number depends on how much time you have for preparing your entries, how much you wish to spend for postage, and how big the prizes are. I usually average about 50-75 in the sweepstakes I enter. I mail about 3 entries per day for sweepstakes of a short (a few weeks) duration. Sweepstakes of 2 or 3 month's duration call for about one or two entries daily. In case it's true that entries received last go in on top and stay there, be sure to save 5 or 10 entries to be mailed on the last few days, including the very last day. Be sure you get them to the post office in time to get them postmarked on the last day.

There are a few sweepstakes that may state in the rules, "only one entry per family." Go ahead and enter anyway. Your odds won't be as good because you can't submit multiple entries, but your chances are as good as anyone else's. On one sweepstakes that I remember, I broke one of my own rules by not reading the sweepstakes rules correctly. They had stated only "one entry per family." Each person that entered was to receive a recipe booklet and money-off coupons. However, I goofed and mailed in about 50 entries. This sponsor must not have kept very close track of how many entries were received from one person because I soon received 50 recipe books and 50 sets of money-off coupons! Each one was mailed separately! But don't count on this happening every time. The best way is to always follow the rules. Should you be picked for a top prize and if the rules state only one entry allowed, you would be disqualified if other entries from you were discovered.

ALL ABOUT MAILING
WHEN TO MAIL YOUR ENTRIES

You should mail entries EVERY day. The best method is to get together all your entries for the month, or for a two-week or a one-week period. Make as many piles of letters as there are days in whatever mailing period you choose. Now take your entries and start distributing them into the different piles. In many sweepstakes, you will have one or more entries that you will want mailed every day. The object is to distribute your entries over the life of the sweepstakes. If the closing date is two months away, you may well want to submit one or more every day. If it's a smaller sweepstakes, one every other day, and so on. The object is to get your entries into as many different mailbags as you can.

Pay attention to any closing dates that will come during the month. Make sure all your entries will be mailed before the deadline, but send them in up to and including the LAST day.

When you finish sorting your entries into different piles for all the days, bundle each one with a rubber band, then take a small piece of paper and put the date for mailing on each bundle. You will now have a bundle for every day! Make sure you mail a bundle every day. If you live in a town where the mail is picked up at different times of the day, vary the time of your mailings. One day, mail it in the morning, then the next day in the afternoon, and so on.

MULTIPLE CHOICE

One type of sweepstakes that you will come across is what I call the multiple choice, or combination entry type sweepstakes, the "Pick the Winner" type sweepstakes would go in this category, too. In regular sweepstakes, the winners are drawn from ALL the entries submitted. In this type however, the winners are drawn from only the CORRECT entries submitted. There will usually be thousands of correct entries, and this type isn't any more difficult than the others. For instance, you may have to pick the winner of the World Series or the winner of a championship football game or a beauty contest. You may have to select the right answer from 4 or 5 listed. The effect of this type of sweepstakes will be to reduce the size of the pool that the winners will finally be drawn from.

The way to enter this type is to use the old saying, "Don't put all your eggs in ONE basket." Put some in EVERY basket. Make sure that you have SOME entries in that winning pool. If it's the football or baseball type, wait until close to the deadline, when the teams are considerably narrowed down to four or six. Then send in some for EACH TEAM. If you have four or five choices, throughout the length of the sweepstakes, enter some for EACH choice. If you think you know which is the right choice, or the winning team, or whatever, go ahead and enter more with your favorite choice. But just be sure that you enter SOME of the other choices, too. It is better to enter 10 entries each of different choices than to enter 100 entries for one choice and have it be wrong.

SHORTCUTS AND TIPS

1. Postage stamps in rolls are the easiest to apply. However, I prefer to use sheets of commemorative stamps which I tear in long strips.

2. Time yourself to determine which is the fastest way for you to address envelopes, by typewriter or by hand. Most of you will probably find it faster by hand. If you do type, roll them through the typewriter in chain fashion.

3. Do one operation at a time to build up speed. If you switch back and forth, first addressing, then making qualifiers, then stuffing, you lose time.

4. If you have children or older folks around, put them all to work! Even small children can lick stamps, stuff envelopes and deposit entries in the mail box. Older children can do block letters, print your name and address on entry blanks, etc. You will find that most of them will love doing it. Your children will get a lot of fun making a scrapbook out of your prize winnings. Save one entry blank or advertisement from a magazine of the sweepstakes. Then, when you win, it can be put in a scrapbook, together with your letter of congratulations.

5. To save time, use abbreviations in YOUR name and address (but NOT in the name and address of the sweepstakes).
   EXAMPLE: R. L. Smith instead of Raymond LeRoy Smith; 2813 E. 19th instead of 2813 East Nineteenth Street; Phila., Pa. instead of Philadelphia, Pennsylvania. (Be sure to include your zip code.)

6. When sealing envelopes in quantity, spread out a dozen or more at a time with the flaps up. Wet a sponge and moisten all the flaps at the same time, then immediately close and seal. The more you do this, the faster you'll become. You can purchase quite cheaply in a stationery supply store, a small envelope moistener. This is a tube that holds water with a small sponge-like material on the end. You simply fill the reservoir and press the spongy end along the flaps.

7. Buy yourself a clipboard so you can address envelopes, make qualifiers, or stick on stamps while sitting in an easy chair watching TV or listening to the radio.

8. If you are sending in an original qualifier, such as a jar label, use this easy method to remove it. Fill the INSIDE of the jar or bottle with hot water. Then put on the lid and immerse it in hot water. In a short time, the label will come off easily in one piece.

9. Try to have a small corner of one room or a desk or small shelf for keeping all your sweepstakes material and supplies in one place. Be organized. Have a notebook to put your sweepstakes magazines in. Punch holes in them and insert them in the notebook. Save large boxes in which envelopes come. When everything is bundled and ready to go, keep them in the boxes and take out just one bundle each day. Use good ball point pens and felt markers. They will make it easier for you.

10. To save time, use labels or a rubber stamp for your return address.

11. In some sweepstakes, you will find different box numbers listed as the sponsor's address in different publications. This is the way the sponsor "keys" his mail to find out which advertisement is best. When you find a sweepstakes like this, mail several entries to EACH box number.

12. Above all, be PERSISTENT. Enter most, if not ALL, the current sweepstakes and enter them consistently. Then you should WIN CONSISTENTLY. You won't win ALL the time, but conversely, the same odds say that you won't lose all the time.

HOW SWEEPSTAKES WINNERS ARE CHOSEN

There is now a profession of sweepstakes judging and many are already involved in it. These judging agencies handle everything involved with sweepstakes. One of the largest is the D. L. Blair Corporation. This one judging agency alone administers several hundred sweepstakes each year! Other agencies that handle sweepstakes are Marden-Kane, Spotts International, I. M. Towers Company, and others.

Some sweepstakes are created by the clients, while many are created by the judging organization itself, then sold to the client. Each sweepstakes has its own set of rules which quite often make it unlike any other sweepstakes.

Most sweepstakes are the random-drawn type. All entries received are put in a giant rotation drum. The winning entries are then drawn, usually by someone who is blindfolded. The first one drawn is the grand prize winner, the second drawn is the second place winner, and so on. In the case where hundreds of thousands of entries are received, it wouldn't be practical to put ALL of them in a drum. Instead, they take a portion of entries received every day or a portion from each full mail bag and these are then put into the drum for the final drawing. This is the reason we urge you to mail entries every day, in an attempt to get at least SOME entries into the final drawing. A little later in this book is an eyewitness account of an actual drawing in progress!

Some sweepstakes use lucky numbers to determine the winners. The winning lucky numbers will be picked by computers. Any remaining prizes after the computer-generated lucky numbers will be picked by the random-drawn method, as nowadays, most all sweepstakes award ALL the prizes.

Entries are usually opened after the drawing, as it would be more expensive to open them before to see if the rules were complied with. If an entry is then found to have violated the rules, or if the postmark is too late, it will be thrown out and another entry drawn until a correct one is found and all prizes awarded.

SWEEPSTAKES JUDGING ORGANIZATIONS

The first thing to keep in mind is that there are SEVERAL judging agencies that administer sweepstakes, and each may employ different procedures, standards, and criteria. For instance, one agency might allow rubber stamps and address labels to be used on the entry blanks when rules say to "hand-print" your name and address. Other agencies may disqualify these. Play it safe and always follow rules <u>exactly</u>.

The following interview is reprinted courtesy of Roger Tyndall. It is from his "CONTEST NEWSLETTER," P. O. Box 1059, Fernandina Beach FL 32034. He has a very impressive publication issued at least 10 times per year. Not only does his bulletin tell about sweepstakes and contests in progress, it also has stories and interviews such as this one. Mr. Tyndall personally interviewed an executive at Marden-Kane, one of the larger agencies that judge sweepstakes and contests. His questions (Q), along with the executive's answers (A) follow:

Q. What is the difference between a contest and a sweepstakes?

A. A contest requires skill in writing a jingle, composing a poem, creating prose, or arriving at a pre-determined answer. A sweepstakes, on the other hand, involves chance and luck based on random selection of entries. No skill is required.

Q. In many cases, do companies spend more on advertising a contest or sweeps than in actual cost of prizes awarded?

A. Generally, yes. Full-page color ads in various magazines are expensive, and, in many cases, advertising expenditures will exceed the cost of prizes.

Q. Why are most sweepstakes and some contests void in a few states?

A. Many states interpret sweepstakes as lotteries, and they feel (rightly or wrongly, depending on your viewpoint) that they are protecting their citizens by restricting sweepstakes...Also (in some states) the proof of purchase laws are so complicated that the company sponsoring a sweepstakes prefers to just stay out of the state altogether and not get involved with complex legal requirements.

Q. What do you do with all those entry forms after a contest closes?

A. We destroy them or return them to our client. Some clients use discarded entries to formulate mailing lists.

Q. How many contests and sweepstakes does your company judge per year?

A. Gee, I don't know. The number of contests and sweeps are decreasing because advertisers are diverting their expenditures to other areas. Contests and sweeps are somewhat cyclical. Some years they're big, and other years, they're not so big.

Q. What percent of winners use official entry forms, and what percent use 3" x 5" cards?

A. I would guess 60% to 70% of winners we select use official entry forms. I guess people feel safer using entry blanks, particularly since they are so readily available.

Q. Do you think it's just as easy to win by using a 3" x 5" card instead of the official entry blank, particularly since entry blanks are harder to get?

A. Yes. And I don't think entry forms are becoming harder to get.

Q. Is it in any way illegal to require an entrant to buy a product as a requirement for submitting an entry?

A. For a sweepstakes, it is illegal to require a purchase as a requisite for submitting an entry. For a contest, however, it is not illegal to require that the entrant make a purchase.

Q. Have you ever disqualified an entry because the entry did not contain what you consider to be "plain block letters?"

A. No. After all, it would be a poor criterion for determining a winner. The writing on the entry must be legible.

Q. How do you pre-select winners by computer?

A. It's a very complex, complicated, technical and sophisticated mathematical formula programmed into the computer.

Q. Do you measure a plain piece of 3" x 5" paper to determine if it is, in fact, precisely 3" x 5"?

A. No. We're just not that technical. If it's 2 feet by 3 feet, we would probably throw it out as not complying with the rules. (EDITOR'S NOTE: Some judging agencies DO measure each 3" x 5" to insure compliance within 1/8" plus or minus.)

Q. After you select a winning entry, do you examine the entry blank closely enough to insure that the form is official and not a counterfeit form? And have you ever uncovered a bogus form?

A. No. We've never discovered a bogus form. We don't consider this to be a problem.

Q. How do you feel about the oddly-shaped, polka-dotted, perfumed, artistic and "creative" envelopes used by some entrants?

A. It's a waste of time. It has no effect on selection procedures. If you reach your hand into the barrel, fish around, and retrieve an envelope while looking the other way, you're not going to see which envelope is covered with polka dots.

Q. What are your selection procedures for picking winners in most sweepstakes?

A. The entry blanks are delivered to several warehouses in various locations here in New York, and then we make random drawings.

Q. Do you make random drawings every day, on certain days, or are drawings made on a random, flexible basis?

A. Strictly on a random basis.

Q. Would you like to describe what you mean in more detail by the term "random drawing?"

A. No.

Q. What federal laws or statutes govern or regulate contests and sweepstakes?

A. The postal laws and postal regulations govern and provide the major guidelines and requirements for planning and conducting sweeps and contests.

Q. Why do you have affidavits of eligibility and release?

A. They fulfill a legal requirement of the sponsor. Also, it assures the sponsor that the entrant or immediate family member is not employed by the sponsoring company, related advertising agency or the contest judging company.

Q. Why do some contests and sweeps have a short time period from the time of public announcement to closing date?

A. It's strictly a matter of fulfilling a particular marketing objective. The object is to quickly generate interest and improve sales. I would say that 60 to 90 days is the industry average.

Q. Several sponsoring companies publish winners' names in newspapers. Why?

A. It is required by some state laws. I believe Florida is one of the states with that requirement.

Q. How many people in the United States are contesters?

A. It would be exceedingly difficult to arrive at that figure, simply because we manage only a portion of the sweeps and contests and there would be so much duplication. I would agree that it is very popular, especially sweeps.

Q. Have you ever selected a winning envelope, only to discover that the entrant forgot to add his name and address on the entry form?

A. I don't believe this has ever happened.

Q. When the rules require the entrant to print in plain block letters the name of the product, should the entrant add quotation marks to enclose the name of the product?

A. This is immaterial.

Q. What are plain block letters?

A. It's simple...just plain block letters. Just make sure they're legible.

Q. Why do you use different post office box numbers for mailing in entries in different ads?

A. This enables the sponsor to determine which sources provide the best return for his advertising expenditure.

Q. Suppose the entry blank I use requires that I return it to P. O. Box 5000, and instead, I mail it into P. O. Box 5001, which I saw in an ad in a magazine for the same sweeps. Would my entry be disqualified if selected?

A. It's possible your entry would be disqualified. I'm not saying for certain that it would be, but always follow rules.

Q. Do you ever spot certain envelopes bearing return addresses that are mailed in in large quantities? In other words, can you spot the "professional" contester?

A. No.

Q. Do sponsors ever request only winners who use their official entry blanks?

A. No. We would never honor such a request.

Q. Why don't more sponsors give winners the choice of accepting the prize or receiving cash?

A. I don't know.

Q. When the Post Office uses a pre-cancelled stamp, how can you verify the postmark date to comply with the rule, "postmarked no later than...etc.?"

A. I don't believe you can. Anyway, the important thing as far as we are concerned is that the entry blank be received by the date specified. That would be the governing factor.

Q. Are you required by law to have available a winner's list?

A. No.

Q. Do you try to achieve any kind of geographical spread of winners?

A. Only if the rules state that that is the objective of the contest. Otherwise, we do not.

Q. If you conduct a contest or sweeps that is repeated every year (e.g. the Benson & Hedges 100's sweeps), do you compare current winners with winners of previous years?

A. No.

Q. Do you maintain winners' lists for comparative purposes.

A. No.

Q. Which is more popular, and which draws the most entries, contests or sweepstakes?

A. Sweepstakes are more popular by far. It takes less time, and it's easier. Also, it's easier and quicker for us to judge, thereby less expensive for the sponsor.

Q. Are the jingles and limericks and essay contests on the decline?

A. No. They are still popular with some sponsors. They were more popular years ago, however.

Q. What time of the year is most popular with the sponsors for introducing contests and sweeps? Which time of the year is least popular?

A. I would say the first and fourth quarters of the calendar year (January, February, March and October, November, December). The first quarter of the year is especially popular, and, I guess that's because people are indoors a lot of the time. The summer is a slow period for contests and sweeps...people away from home and it's the traditional vacation period.

Q. What state produces the most entries?

A. California.

Q. Does it matter how you address the envelope in which you mail your entry--all capital letters or a combination of capital letters and lower letters?

A. It's really immaterial.

Q. Does it matter how you write the address to which you mail your entry--P. O. Box, Post Office Box, Box, POB, Bx, etc.?

A. Really, it's immaterial. Just have the correct address.

Q. If the contestant uses a 3" x 5" card instead of the official entry blank, is he bound by the rules stated on official entry blank?

A. Yes.

Q. Do you advise companies on how to prepare their contest or sweeps?

A. Yes. We advise them on how to plan, write the rules, execute the art work, prepare promotional material...all sorts of services in addition to just selecting the winners.

Q. Have past increases in postage rates affected the number of entries?

A. No, it has not had a significant effect on the number of entries.

Q. Why do some companies prefer to do their own judging instead of utilizing your services?

A. I don't know.

Q. Does it matter if the 3" x 5" card or piece of paper is ruled or plain?

A. No.

Q. Colored or white?

A. Immaterial.

Q. Who does your recipe judging?

A. We don't have any. They seem to be becoming more popular.

Q. When writing the name of the product on a 3" x 5" card, and the name of the product requires more than one word, does it matter if all the words are written on one line or several lines?

A. It doesn't matter.

Q. Are you or the sponsoring companies in any way concerned about the "professional" contester?

A. No. We have no way of determining who is or who is not a "pro."

Q. What advice do you have for contesters?

A. Follow the rules.

Q. What is the largest number of entries you have received in a single sweeps or contest?

A. We received about 1½ million entries in one particular sweeps.

Q. If a contest or sweeps rule limits entry to one per person or household, how do you verify this?

A. Actually, you can't. Not too many sweeps have this rule.

Q. Do people ever write in thanking you for selecting their entry?

A. Yes...occasionally.

Q. Does it help to have name and return address on the outside of the envelope?

A. Immaterial.

Q. If you're asked to add the name of establishment where you made a purchase of the sponsor's product (usually the name of the store and the store manager), and you omit this, would your entry be disqualified?

A. If the sponsor wants to award a duplicate prize or alternate prize to the store manager, I would recommend that you include the name of the store and the name of the manager.

Q. Do you receive many requests for winners' lists, and why don't you print the entire address of the winners?

A. We don't receive too many requests. We try to protect the winners from harassment. Of course, this provides only limited protection. Nevertheless, the objective is to protect the winner.

Q. Who wins most...women or men?

A. Women. They submit most of the entries.

END OF INTERVIEW

In addition to his interesting interview with Marden-Kane, Roger Tyndall also observed another sweepstakes judging agency in operation. He received permission to observe the selection of winners in the Peter Paul "Indescribably Delicious" Sweepstakes administered by the judging agency Spotts International, St. Paul, Minnesota. His observations follow:

In one end of the conference room there were 49 large, canvas mail sacks. Each mail sack was full. These sacks contained the 103,939 entries submitted in this sweepstakes. Next to the sacks was a cylindrical, metal selection drum. Into the drum was placed 49 small slips of paper numbered sequentially 1 through 49, which represented a correspondingly numbered mail sack.

To select the grand prize winner, an account executive for Spotts was tightly blindfolded and led to the selection drum. A Pinkerton guard rotated the drum several times to insure random selection. The executive then reached through the hinged opening at the top of the drum and retrieved a single piece of paper. It was number 39.

The executive, still blindfolded, was then led over to mail sack number 39. She reached in and pulled out a small, white envelope measuring 3-5/8" x 6-1/2". This envelope was handed to the President of Spotts International. He first checked the postmark to insure compliance with the 30 June closing date. When asked if he was interested in how the envelope was addressed, he said "no." "If the envelope reaches us, that's all that counts," he said.

After checking the postmark, he opened the envelope. The winning entry was submitted on a plain, white, 3" x 5" card, along with a 3" x 5" card on which was printed "Peter Paul." The prize was a Dodge van valued at $7,500.00 plus a $2,500.00 gift certificate. (Other winners in this sweepstakes were selected from ALL 49 mail sacks, not just #39 from which the grand prize was selected.)

When a selected envelope was opened, each 3" x 5" card or piece of paper was measured carefully to insure compliance with the official rules. They allowed for a tolerance of plus or minus 1/8". Of the approximately 275 entries selected, 18 were disqualified! The reasons: incorrect size of the 3" x 5"; using a rubber stamp to indicate name & address when the rules required entrant to "print" that information; writing in a script style instead of printing; entries postmarked after June 30 closing date; failure to indicate on the entry form the name and address of store where entry was obtained (Official rules clearly read "Incomplete entries will be ineligible"); and other reasons.

A couple of other interesting points Mr. Tyndall found out from Spotts: Entries are NOT disqualified at Spotts if entrant doesn't indicate his telephone number when that information is requested...after all, the entrant may not have a telephone. However, they do prohibit address labels on entry blanks IF the rules require entrant to "print" his name and address. If the rules state "complete" the entry form, you may use address labels.

Over half of the entries were submitted the last two weeks of the sweepstakes, which was said by Spotts to be typical. The majority of the winners used 3"x5" pieces of paper or 3"x5" cards instead of the official entry blank. Only a small number of the winning entries contained a Peter Paul candy wrapper. Most winners used a substitute 3"x5" for the required candy wrapper.

The most important lesson learned from the drawing...FOLLOW THE RULES!!

LETTERS OF CONGRATULATIONS

When you win a prize in a sweepstakes, you will be notified by an eagerly awaited letter of congratulations. It can come anywhere from two weeks to two months after the sweepstakes closes. The letter can come either from the sponsor or the judging organization.

A typical letter is as follows:

> Dear Winner:
>
> Congratulations! Your name has been drawn as one of the Third Prize Winners in the (Brand Name) Sweepstakes. You have won a 19" RCA TV.
>
> Enclosed is a certificate of compliance with the official rules. Will you kindly complete this form, attesting to the fact that neither you nor any member of your immediate family is an employee of the sponsor, its advertising agency, judging agency, or any organization participating in the sweepstakes.
>
> We would like to congratulate you on your good fortune and hope that you will be pleased with your prize. Arrangements are being made to have your prize shipped directly to you at your present address. In the event you have moved from your present address, please advise immediately as to where the prize should be shipped.
>
> Our sincere congratulations on your fortune are extended, with hopes for your continued good luck.
>
> We wish to take this opportunity to thank you for participating in the (Brand Name) sweepstakes and we sincerely hope that you will continue to enjoy (Brand Name).
>
> Yours very truly,

It usually requires from 4 to 8 weeks after notification to receive your prize, as stated in the letter.

If you're the type of person who writes thank-you notes, why not write one to the sponsor to thank him for the prize. If you were introduced to the product for the first time, let him know this. He will appreciate your letter and if enough of them are received, it could influence him to use sweepstakes as a promotion again.

AFFIDAVITS AND INVESTIGATIONS

If the prize that you win is a large one, the sponsor or judging organization may make an investigation and/or have you fill out an affidavit and have it notarized. This investigation could be done through a telephone call, by a personal interview or filling out necessary forms received in the mail.

The purpose of this investigation is simply to ascertain that you followed the rules, were eligible to enter, and aren't related to the sponsor, his advertising agency or judging organization. Maybe the rules stated the entrant must be over 21, be a woman, a pet owner or some other stipulated qualification. The investigation will make sure you fully complied and are eligible under the rules.

TAXES

This book wouldn't be complete without a section on paying income taxes on the prizes that you win. Some of you may be saying, "Let me win the prize before I worry about paying taxes." But the time will come when you will want to refer to this section.

Tax laws change from time to time, and different individuals in various circumstances may alter the way in which they figure their tax and apply tax laws to themselves. So for the final word, you should consult your local agent of the Internal Revenue Service, tax professionals such as H & R Block, or a current tax guide. Generally speaking, the following should apply. You declare the fair market value of your winnings, less the expenses incurred in winning them.

Even though you consider entering sweepstakes as a hobby, you must pay taxes on any income or prizes that you make from it. However, if you have a net loss, you cannot declare it.

On your Federal Income Tax Return, under the classification, "Income from sources other than wages, etc." On the line marked "Miscellaneous Income" you state "Net income from sweepstakes - Schedule Attached." On a separate piece of paper, you then put your name and address as shown on your return. You then state your gross income from prizes. Then list the expenses that you incurred in winning these prizes. Subtract these expenses from the gross, and you have your NET income.

FAIR MARKET VALUE

Many sweepstakes award merchandise prizes instead of cash. The sponsor in his promotion may advertise that the prizes are worth X amount of dollars. However, this stated amount may be inflated and may not represent what you would actually pay for the item at retail. Therefore, you should only pay taxes on the "fair market value." It has been defined as "the price which a willing seller, not compelled to sell, will take, and a willing purchaser, not compelled to buy, will pay."

If the merchandise prize is one that you don't wish to keep, sell it. It should be a bona fide sale to a bona fide purchaser. The amount that you report on your Income Tax Return is the proceeds from this sale. Any expenses such as newspaper advertisements may be deducted from the gross selling price to arrive at net proceeds.

If you keep the prize, you will then declare the fair market value. Naturally, you want this to be as low as possible, and you should have proof as the stated price of the article obtained from any legitimate sources. One good way to prove the fair market value is from newspaper clippings. Watch your papers for sales on the article that you won, then clip this and save it. Other ways are direct mail advertisements, catalogue listings, or by having it appraised. Be honest. Do not expect to show a letter or bill from a friendly dealer with a price that he would not offer to all his customers.

Some sponsors have been known to pay the taxes on your prize, although this would be the exception and not the rule. If you are a recipient of this generosity, remember that any money received as reimbursement for taxes on prizes is income itself and must be declared as such on your return.

EXPENSES IN SWEEPSTAKES

Some of the expenses you may list as deductible are postage, stationery supplies, (envelopes, pens, pads of paper, address stickers, rubber stamps, ink pads, etc.) and subscriptions to sweepstakes magazines. The cost of sweepstakes books, such as this one, is deductible too, if they have a so-called "short" life, as compared to books with a long-life expectancy.

When you buy postage, give the clerk a piece of paper with your name and address and the quantity and value of stamps that you are purchasing. He will date this by rubber stamp. Do the same for any postal cards or stamped envelopes that you purchase for sweepstakes. However, the burden will be on you to show that you used the postage for entering sweepstakes, and not for your own personal use paying bills, writing letters, etc. You should keep all receipts and bills for your supplies.

You cannot deduct the cost of a product that you may have purchased to obtain the label or box top if the product would be useful to you. This would be considered as a personal expense. But remember, as I have stated earlier in the book, IT IS NOT NECESSARY TO PURCHASE THE PRODUCTS in order to win the prizes. Block letters will win just as easily.

SWEEPSTAKES PUBLICATIONS

You will probably want to subscribe to one or more publications devoted exclusively to sweepstakes and contests. They will give you all the information about the various sweepstakes and contests in progress. You won't find out about ALL of them otherwise, because you won't come across ALL the entry blanks in your store, or read ALL the magazines that sweepstakes may be advertised in. The average person doesn't realize that there may be as many as 30 or 40 sweepstakes and contests in progress at any given time!

Following are some names and addresses of several bulletins and newsletters. They are issued anywhere from 10 to 12 times per year. You'll find the subscription rates quite reasonable for all the information they give you. They will be glad to send you a sample copy of their publication and subscription information if you send them 50¢ plus a large, self-addressed, stamped envelope.

Contest News-Letter
Dept. RD2
PO Box 1059
Fernandina Beach FL 32034

Golden Chances
Dept. RD2
PO Box 655
South Pasadena CA 91030

Benro Enterprises
Dept. RD2
PO Box 6656
Philadelphia PA 19149

National Sweepstakes Guide
Dept. RD2
PO Box 261
Lansdowne PA 19050

Sweepstakes Newsletter
Dept. RD2
PO Box F
Andover NJ 07821

Contest Hotline
Dept. RD2
PO Box 1255
Chico CA 95927

Contest Bulletin
Eggleston Enterprises
Dept. RD2
Milford NY 13807

In addition to putting out monthly information, Eggleston Enterprises also sells labels and entry blanks. But as we said before, IT IS NOT NECESSARY to use the actual labels or boxtops in order to win prizes. However, some sweepstakes require the use of the OFFICIAL ENTRY BLANK only.

While not having anything to do with sweepstakes, if you are interested in receiving a free list of puzzle contest sponsors, send a large, self-addressed stamped envelope to:

R & D Services
P. O. Box 644-R
Des Moines, Iowa 50303

TYPICAL QUESTIONS AND ANSWERS

Q. Do I need to use "quote marks" around the required word or phrases that I put in block letters?

A. No, you do not. With or without is O.K.

Q. Why are there different box numbers on sweepstakes notices in different advertisements, entry blanks, etc.?

A. This is the way the sponsor "keys" his advertisements, to check the results on the different promotional methods.

Q. If the rules state, "a plain piece of paper", without specifying size, what size should I use?

A. Any size is permissible. I like to use large sheets.

Q. If the rules state, "plain paper or a postcard", which is best?

A. Plain paper in a large envelope.

Q. How are sweepstakes winners chosen?

A. Most are chosen by blindfold random drawing.

Q. If the pads of paper I buy to use as qualifiers are not exactly 3" x 5", would this disqualify me?

A. Variations up to 1/8" should be acceptable. Some rules even state "approximately 3" x 5"." I would try to use as close to 3" x 5" as possible.

Q. What are my odds in winning a sweepstakes prize?

A. Your actual numerical odds depend upon how many entries are received and how many entries you submit. If there were 100,000 submitted and

10 of them were yours, your chances would be 10,000 to 1. If you submitted 100, your chances would be 1,000 to 1. So you see, the more entries you submit, the better your chances of winning.

Q. In some sweepstakes that I see advertised in magazines, it states that you must use the "Official Entry Blank", yet I cannot find any in the stores. Why doesn't my local store carry these blanks? Where can I obtain them?

A. If the product that sponsors the sweepstakes is sold in your local stores, you can be sure that someone in the store is receiving them, but for one reason or another, not putting them out. Talk to your grocer. Tell him you're interested in them and tell him to put them out. Another possible way to obtain them is by writing to the sponsor. Another good source is Eggleston Enterprises, Milford, New York 13807.

Q. Is it right to send more than one entry in an envelope so I can save postage?

A. Most sweepstakes rules plainly state, "only one entry per envelope." But even if they don't, winners are usually drawn before the envelopes are opened so you could have a hundred entry blanks in one envelope and it could count as just one.

Q. I am an older person, and I can't print very well. The requirement for block letters worries me. I don't enter some sweepstakes for fear of being disqualified. How strict is judging on the neatness of block letters?

A. The rules do not state that the block letters have to be perfect. Judges are aware of this situation and are lenient. The term "block letters" is commonly taken to mean, "no script." A small child learning to print could well make acceptable block letters; in fact, my own have!

Q. Can my family win more than one prize in a single sweepstakes if the rules do not say, "ONLY one prize per family?"

A. Yes, it happens many times.

Q. If you don't need the sponsor's label or wrapper to win, how can the sponsor make any money?

A. Sweepstakes have a big drawing power, and millions of entries are sometimes received. Advertising agencies and sponsors know even if you don't buy their product for the label that you will have been subjected to a mild form of brainwashing when you wrote their product name many times in block letters. If you write a product name over and over 10, 50 or a hundred times when you go to the store to actually purchase the type of product, there is a good chance you will buy the sponsor's. It has been proven that sales go up during sweepstakes, or else there would not be so many. Also, a certain percentage of people still believe you have a better chance to win with a real qualifier and they do buy the product.

Q. Can I use a 3" x 5" file card when the rules state, "use a 3" x 5" plain piece of paper?

A. I have won using file cards and other have, too. I don't use them exclusively, however, as they are more expensive than plain paper. When I do use them, it's usually to give more weight or substance to my entry, or when the rules state to use a 3" x 5" <u>card</u>.

Q. Has a survey ever been taken to determine if the BIG prize winners use actual qualifiers or block letter qualifiers?

A. Not that I now of. However, a survey is NOT NEEDED. I have won major prizes with block letter qualifiers and so have others I know. Actual qualifiers would make the cost of the entries prohibitive. The postal inspectors would have stopped these promotional sweepstakes years ago if anything were dishonest.

Q. Is there any difference between the wordings, "use block lettering" and "use plain block letters?"

A. There is no difference.

Q. Can I use one piece of paper instead of two, by hand printing my name on one side and putting the block letters on the other side?

A. No. Use one piece for your name and another for the qualifier, unless the rules clearly state to put them both together on ONE piece of paper.

Q. The rules often state, "Use a plain piece of paper." Could I use lined paper, such as notebook paper?

A. I would not recommend it. I always use unlined paper.

Q. Could the envelopes I use for the sweepstakes have my return address printed on them?

A. Yes, they could. However, they are more expensive than return address labels or a rubber stamp. Actually, no return address need be used at all.

Q. Is it all right to buy the box tops to use as qualifiers from one of the companies that specialize in this?

A. It's been done for years. After all, someone had to buy it originally. However, if you need the type of product, buy at least one. Remember, no purchase of product is necessary.

Q. I have heard that if you win a big prize, there is sometimes an investigation made. What is this for?

A. To be sure that you are not related in any way to the advertising agency that promoted the sweepstakes, the sponsor or the company that judges the sweepstakes.

Q. Can I use carbon paper to make multiple entries?

A. I wouldn't recommend it. I always do each entry, qualifier and envelope separately. However, I have known someone else to use carbon paper occasionally.

Q. My husband operates a small grocery store. If he sells a product whose company is offering a sweepstakes, can we still enter?

A. Yes, you can enter as long as you are not related or EMPLOYED by the sponsoring company, advertising agency or judging agency.

IN CLOSING

By now you should have all the information you need to enter sweepstakes intelligently. So get busy and start entering. You won't win in every sweepstakes, but if you enter consistently, you should win prizes consistently. I averaged about three prizes per month over a period of 18 months. All your wins may not be big prizes, but there is still a thrill of winning and knowing that you may win the "big one," while the smaller prizes keep coming in. Even figuring today's postage rates, if you send in 100 entries, it's a pretty good investment risk, considering that the top prize may very well be worth $25,000 or $30,000. Even if the postage rates go up, which they have a habit of doing from time to time like everything else, don't let that keep you from entering. It may very well be the best time to enter as the general public, for a while after rates are increased, may not send in as many entries, increasing your chances to win!

Good luck! And remember, ANYONE CAN WIN SWEEPSTAKES!